I CAN'T BREATHE

I CAN'T BREATHE

DON'T DIE TWICE

DEBORAH LASTER

TABLE OF CONTENTS

Introduction   7

Chapter One
I CAN'T BREATHE   10

Chapter Two
THE CURSES OF DEUTERONOMY   19

Chapter Three
BIBLICAL HISTORY OF
"I CAN'T BREATHE"   45

Chapter Four
SLAVERY IN AMERICA   57

Chapter Five
WHY WAS ISRAEL ENSLAVED?   63

Chapter Six
WHO IS THE TRUE NATION OF ISRAEL?   67

Chapter Seven
WHO ARE THE JEWS IN ISRAEL?   69

Chapter Eight
THE REAL ENEMY - SATAN   73

Chapter Nine
THE VALLEY OF DRY BONES   79

Chapter Ten
UNDERSTANDING OUR ROLE IN CHRIST 83
Chapter Eleven
BREATHE AGAIN 91
Chapter Twelve
THE PRODIGAL SON 99
Chapter Thirteen
MY JOURNEY 103
The Israelite Man - Poem 108
FINAL WORDS FROM THE AUTHOR 109

Connect with the Author 115

INTRODUCTION

The Bible is a history book about the ancestors of Black people of great and diverse nationalities. Unfortunately, the world (this Beast/Babylonian government system) has given us a false narrative of who we are. We often hear the phrase *the system*, but do we know what *the system* is all about?

God wants to expose the lies embedded in the fabric of our society. History is NOT as we have come to know it. It has been rewritten by those who rule this world (Rome/Elite). Secret societies have been established throughout the earth. The secret is to keep us from the truth. What truth? **That we are the Chosen People of the Most High God!** These *secret societies*, or the elitists, have evolved the whole world into a flux of change. The world has veered away from traditional values, moral standards, cultural norms, and beliefs. We have forgotten God's laws and commandments.

The elitists are pushing for globalization (the growing interdependence of the world's economies, cultures, and populations) and conformity (the process whereby people change their beliefs, attitudes, actions, or perceptions to match more closely those held by groups). The truth of the matter is that the global policy of the world today is the pressure to conform. Globalization is a movement of conformity. Globalization says, "Everyone must conform to the same thing! Get in line or get out! Be like everyone else, or don't be!" Conformity cancels uniqueness and distinction. It demands the surrender of your convictions, values, beliefs, principles, morality, and honor. Conformity says, "Forget what you believe and accept what *we* believe!" It implies that you must forget what you consider your culture and accept *their* culture.

The goal of globalization is for all nations, societies, cultures, people, and all communities to be a "one-world system." **Wake up, people! Understand the truth about the world and system that has so cunningly beguiled us!** Revelations 12:9 tells us, "The Devil, who is called Satan, deceived the whole world."

We have become a people who are the epitome of selfishness, arrogance, and ignorance and have the unmitigated gall to tell an omnipotent, omnipresent, omniscient God, who owns the world and everything in it, that we are more knowledgeable than Him and don't need Him. THIS is why we have been constantly abused, exploited, killed, and destroyed by America and other nations. THIS is why we cry, *"I can't breathe."* We must return to the Most High God and begin following His laws, statutes, and commandments. The Word of the LORD says in Deuteronomy 30:19, "I have set before you, life and death." Then HE simply tells us, "Now choose life so that you and your children may live and that you may love the LORD your God, listen to His voice, and hold fast to him." Then He will breathe life into our dry bones.

This book will take you on a journey, identifying who we are as the true people of God, the promised people of the Bible, God's chosen people. The time has come to awake, children of the Most High. The time has come to *breathe*. You don't have to die twice.

CHAPTER ONE

I CAN'T BREATHE

Death is inevitable. Man is appointed to die and face judgment. Today, people are dying at a rapid rate. For those who have already gone before us, I have often wondered whether they made peace with the Creator God and entered the Kingdom of Heaven. I sometimes think about people clinging to their very lives, being presented with the reality that this could be their last breath and knowing that they are ever so close to losing their lives. Do they think to call out to the name above every name, *the name of Jesus?* In Luke 23, the Bible speaks of two thieves crucified with Christ, one on His right and the other on His left. One of the thieves had no desire to cry out to Christ, for he had no reverence for Christ. Yet, the other thief apparently thought to himself, *since I am going to die and have nothing to lose, I will cry out to Him.* He understood that this man is the Christ, and showing reverence for Christ, asks Jesus to remember him when He comes into the Kingdom. Jesus says to him, "Truly, you will be with me in paradise." What do you have to lose to acknowledge Him and ask Him to save you from a second death? This is a plea to consider your ways and change your thinking, ideology, and philosophy so that you may live and not die. In the unfortunate event that you become the next hashtag saying, "*I can't breathe*," you do NOT have to die twice.

Unfortunately, the plight of Black people and the outcry "I CAN'T BREATHE" has been a significant component since slavery. Unfortunately, most Americans are in blatant denial of the existence of the plight of Black people, as we know it now to be—systemic or institutional racism (relating to discriminatory laws and regulations embedded in a society or organization against a particular group of people). Since many are oblivious to systemic racism after 400 years of slavery, we find ourselves back in the clutches of being killed at an astronomical rate for simply being *Black*. Let's consider our ways and remember those whose breath was taken away within seconds or minutes, mainly those under the age of fifty years. We pray they are all at peace with the LORD, but no one knows anyone's plight after death but Christ. Here are just a few:

ERIC GARNER July 17, 2014, Eric Garner died in the New York borough of Staten Island after Daniel

Pantaleo, a New York City Police Department (NYPD) officer, placed his arm around Garner's neck and wrestled him to the ground. With multiple officers pinning him down, Garner repeated the words *"I can't breathe"* 11 times while lying face down on the sidewalk.

GEORGE FLOYD May 25, 2020, after a store clerk allegedly said he had passed a counterfeit $20 bill in Minneapolis, police officer Derek Chauvin knelt on Floyd's neck for a period initially reported to be 8 minutes and 46 seconds. George warned the police that he would die because he couldn't breathe.

MANUEL ELLIS June 3, 2020, Manuel Ellis of Tacoma, Washington, 33 years old, a black man who called out *"I can't breathe"* before dying in police custody, was killed as a result of oxygen deprivation and physical restraint.

CHRISTOPHER LOWE July 26, 2018, Christopher Lowe died while handcuffed in the back of a police cruiser in Fort Worth, Texas. When Lowe told officers he was dying and could not breathe, officers told him, "Don't pull that shit," berated him, and threatened to pepper spray him.

JAVIER AMBER II At 40 years old, Amber died following a police encounter in March 2019, crying, *"I can't breathe."* He died in Austin, Texas, following a vehicle chase.

JOHN ELLIOTT NEVILLE Neville died in Winston-Salem, North Carolina, on December 2, 2019, after being restrained in the Forsyth County jail. During a medical emergency, he behaved erratically. He said, "I can't breathe" at least ten times, as well as "help me," while he was in a prone restraint.

BYRON WILLIAMS September 5, 2019, Byron Williams, age 50, was arrested by Las Vegas police for riding his bicycle without a safety light. Less than an hour later, he was dead. Body camera video showed the officers chasing Williams, holding him on the ground, handcuffed, and kneeling on his back before lifting him upright and dragging him away. Williams repeatedly told officers, *"I can't breathe."* He said it at least 17 times.

DERRICK SCOTT Scott, an Oklahoma man, age 42, told a police officer, "I can't breathe" before dying. The officer responded, "I don't care." Video of the 2019 incident shows officers restraining Scott, who is heard repeatedly asking for his medicine and saying, *"I can't breathe."*

ELIJAH MCCLAIN McClain, a 23-year-old Black man, was approached by police officers in Aurora, Colorado, as he walked home from a convenience store. The officers tackled McClain to the ground and put him in a carotid hold. On recordings, he can be heard saying several times, *"I can't breathe."*

CLYDE R. KERR III Kerr, 43, was a godly, honorable man who could be labeled as a martyr, Army Veteran, and a Black Lafayette Parish Sheriff Deputy in Louisiana. He condemned police brutality and institutional racism. He described his struggle as a Black law enforcement officer in a system that he said condones police brutality against Black people. He died from a self-inflicted gunshot wound to the head. Clyde was saying, "*I can't breathe.*"

According to a 2020 report by the New York Times, over 70 people who died in police custody used this phrase. When someone says, "*I can't breathe,*" we literally understand that they CANNOT breathe. However, when looking at this phrase on a broader scale, I would dare to say that not only are those having a knee on their necks crying out, "*I can't breathe.*" I believe those being choked to death also cry out, "*I can't breathe.*" If we could see this from another perspective, I would dare to say the infants incubating in the wombs of women, being sacrificed on the altars of planned parenthood, are crying out, "*I can't breathe.*" The kid in the inner city, running from being chased by the cop or by a rival gang, is crying out, "*I can't breathe.*" The women being murdered in domestic violence are crying out, "*I can't breathe.*" Children being mentally, sexually, and physically abused in their homes are crying out, "*I can't breathe.*" Our women and children kidnapped in sex trafficking are crying out, *"I can't breathe."* Random people dying in the hospital with various illnesses and diseases are crying out, *"I can't breathe."* Black people, by the mere fact of the color of their skin, are randomly saying, **"I CAN'T BREATHE!"**

One might inquire why so many people, especially Blacks, find themselves in complicated, dangerous, indefensible, and chaotic situations in which they are at the mercy of another, crying out, "I can't breathe." Is this something that has recently developed? Is it new, or has this spoken or sometimes unspoken phrase always been around? Well, let's rewind down memory lane, or better yet, reach back into history.

Hosea 4:6 says, "My people are destroyed for lack of knowledge: because thou hast rejected knowledge, I will also reject thee, that thou shalt be no priest to me: seeing thou has forgotten the law of thy God, I will also forget thy children."

Who is being destroyed for lack of knowledge? Who is Hosea referring to? What group of people have been literally and systematically destroyed in this country? The answer is those of a darker hue or complexion. The following questions would be: Why have these people been targeted for destruction? Why does God call them *His people*? What knowledge do they lack? Why are Black People crying, *"I can't breathe,"* while being systematically destroyed?

Deuteronomy 28 outlines the blessing and curses that will come upon the people of God who do not follow His laws. In the book of Deuteronomy, the God of all creation prophesied the end-time prophecy about God's chosen people and how they will live because they disobeyed God.

They (His people) have roused my jealousy by worshiping things that are not God; they have provoked my anger with their useless idols. Now I will rouse their jealousy through people who are not even a people. I will provoke them (His people) to anger with a foolish nation (United States).

Deuteronomy 32:21

But it shall come to pass, if thou wilt not hearken unto the voice of the LORD thy God, to observe to do all his commandments and his statutes which I command thee this day; that all these curses shall come upon thee and overtake thee.

Deuteronomy 28:15

We know, according to Genesis 9: 21-25, that Noah's grandson, Canaan, was cursed when his father, Ham, saw Noah's nakedness. As a result of this, Noah cursed Ham's son, Canaan. This curse was not placed on ALL darker-skinned people. It was only put on those who are the descendants of Canaan. The curse stated in Deuteronomy 28:15 was a result of our people, who are the descendants of Shem, who engaged in constant rebellion and sin against the Almighty God.

If you refuse to listen to the LORD your God and to obey the commands and decrees, he has given you, all these curses will pursue and overtake you until you are destroyed. These horrors will serve as a sign and warning among you and your descendants forever."

Deuteronomy 28:45-46

We are NOT cursed because of the LIE that we are the descendants of Ham, but because we continue to disobey the Laws of the Almighty God. We were sold to our enemies because we provoked the Holy One of Israel by sacrificing unto devils and NOT the Most High.

NOTES

CHAPTER TWO

THE CURSES OF DEUTERONOMY

The true children of God were warned by The Holy One that if we continued in our disobedience and sin, we would suffer the curses of Deuteronomy 28:15-68, hence why *we can't breathe*. In this chapter, we will explore the details of each curse as outlined in the Bible.

1. Slavery and Captivity

Thou shall beget sons and daughters, but thou shalt not enjoy them; for they shall go into captivity.

Deuteronomy 28:41

The scripture above is self-explanatory. No group can fit these scriptures other than Black Americans and those sold along the coast in slavery. It is a known fact that slavery broke up families, and children were also enslaved. It was common in slavery to see young boys and girls, even babies, taken from their parents to be sold to sexually abusive slave masters. We know our sons and daughters were taken from our ancestors and sold to the highest bidder. Joel 3:3 states, "They traded boys to obtain prostitutes and sold girls for enough wine to get drunk."

When the White patriarch died, his property— including Black slaves—was cruelly divided among all his children or to anyone else and sold off without reservation. Black slave families were destroyed and splintered into oblivion whenever a *master* died.

The LORD will bring a distant nation against you from the end of the earth, and it will swoop down on you like a vulture. It is a nation whose language you do not understand, a fierce and heartless nation that shows no respect for the old and no pity for the young.

Deuteronomy 28: 49-50

We were brought into a nation *as swift as the eagle flieth* (The eagle refers to several countries, notably the United States and the European Union)—a nation whose tongue thou shalt not understand. We were brought over from the coast of Africa, and we did not speak the English language. Slaves did not know the language of their oppressors or the language of the land they were sold into. Several nations participated in capturing and selling Black slaves. These people had no regard/sympathy for our newborns or our elderly. Slave masters did not show any favors to women, children, or old or young slaves. Everyone was regarded as property, like cattle. Western civilization was built on the sweat, blood, and tears of black men, women, and children, who planted, cultivated, picked, and wrapped cotton into 200-pound bales.

Black children who were toddlers themselves had to take care of White babies. Black Slave women who were nursing were forced into being *wet nannies*. It was mandated that the Slave woman use one breast for the white baby and the other for her black child, or her black baby sometimes died because she could not nurse them at all. If the slave woman was caught nursing her black baby on the same breast she nursed the white baby, she was whipped because it was similar to Blacks and Whites sharing the same drinking fountain.

2. Powerless Against Our Enemy

The LORD will cause you to be defeated by your enemies. You will attack your enemies from one direction, but you will scatter from them in seven! You will be an object of horror to all the kingdoms of the earth.

Deuteronomy 28:41

In Africa and Arabia, our enemies (Arab invaders, neighboring African Tribes, European nations, and European Judaism converts called "Jews") came against us, capturing us, killing us, or driving us from one habitat to the next, which caused our people to be removed into all the kingdoms of the earth. If it weren't for the Jewish-European and Arab involvement in the slave trades in Africa, we would still have a little of our past heritage today. These two nations also forced their religious beliefs on Blacks, killing, enslaving, and raping them in the process.

There have been many revolts by our people, including (a) the 1791-1804 Haitian Revolution in Saint-Domingue, (b) the 1800 slave rebellion by Gabriel Prosser in Virginia, (c) Nat Turner's 1831 rebellion in Virginia, and (d) John Brown's 1859 raid in Virginia. These acts were against those who held them in captivity; however, they were overpowered and did not prevail. One of the largest slave insurrections in the history of the U.S. began in Louisiana Territory in 1811. After the defeat, many of the 500 rebelling enslaved people were mutilated, decapitated, and burned alive.

There among those nations you will find no peace or place to rest. And the LORD will cause your heart to tremble, your eyesight to fail, and your soul to despair.
Deuteronomy 28:65

Blacks scattered around the world were economically, educationally, socially, and politically suppressed in whatever land they lived. Black people worked endlessly daily, building these United States and other nations for our captives. They found no peace or place to rest.

The foreigners living among you will become stronger and stronger, while you become weaker and weaker. They will lend money to you, but you will not lend to them. They will be the head, and you will be the tail!

Deuteronomy 28:43

Every nation of people living among us has risen above us as we continue to remain at the bottom. Black people have borrowed money from every other nation, and we primarily work for every other nation. We are constantly borrowing their money yet have none to lend.

3. Sent To Egypt <u>Again</u> by Ship

And the LORD shall bring thee into Egypt (tribulation/bondage/misery) again with ships, by the way whereof I spake unto thee, thou shalt see it no more again: and there ye shall be sold unto your enemies for bondmen and bondwomen, and no man shall buy (redeem) you.

Deuteronomy 28:68

Why does Deuteronomy 28:68 say, "And the LORD shall bring thee into Egypt again with ships?" First and foremost, we, Black Americans, are the ONLY group that was brought into a strange land by ships. The scripture goes on to say, *"into Egypt again."* This lets me know that if we are going to

Egypt again, we must have experienced Egypt in the past. Egypt means *bondage*. The question is, **when were we in Egypt or bondage?**

And the Egyptians made the children of Israel to serve with rigor: And they made their lives bitter with hard bondage, in mortar, and in brick, and in all manner of service in the field: all their service, wherein they made them serve, was with rigor.

Exodus 1:13

This scripture says that the Children of Israel (Black people) served the Egyptians rigorously. We were the people back then in Egypt; we are the people now in Egypt (America).

I realize that our first Egypt (tribulation/bondage misery) was with the Egyptians, and now, our second Egypt is here in the United States. The scripture says, "And the LORD shall bring thee into Egypt or bondage again with ships." The United States is the country we came into again in ships as slaves into bondage.

The first British slave ship to reach the Americas was called *Jesus of Lubeck*, a 700-ton vessel. Between 1562 and 1567, Britain's first slave trader John Hawkins profited so greatly from the slave trade that it caught the Queen's attention. She donated the Jesus of Lubeck and another ship called *The Minion* as an investment into Hawkins' slave trade enterprise. Sir John Hawkins was *supposedly* a religious gentleman who insisted that his crew *serve God daily* and love one another.

4. Scattered Among All Nations

For the Lord will scatter you among the nations, where only a few of you will survive. There, in a foreign land, you will worship idols made from wood and stone—gods that neither see nor hear nor eat nor smell.

Deuteronomy 4:27

And the LORD will scatter you among all the nations from one end of the earth to the other. There you will worship foreign gods that neither you nor your ancestors have known gods made of wood and stone!

Deuteronomy 28:64

I will scatter you among the nations and bring out my sword against you. Your land will become desolate, and your cities will lie in ruins.

Leviticus 26:33

The Lord will uproot the people of Israel from this good land (Jerusalem) that he gave their ancestors and will scatter them beyond the Euphrates River.

1 Kings 14:15

Please remember what you told your servant Moses: "If you are unfaithful to me, I will scatter you among the nations."

Nehemiah 1:8

*I will scatter them around the world, in places they
and their ancestors never heard of ...*

Jeremiah 9:16

*And when I scatter them among the nations, they will
know that I am the Lord.*

Ezekiel 12:15

*I will scatter you among the nations and purge you of
your wickedness.*

Ezekiel 22:15

In 70 A.D., Rome brought a temporary end to
the Nation of Israel, burning the city of Jerusalem,
bringing a great sword and slaughter. Roman hatred
for Israel and vengeance on its people was so great
that, over time, Israel migrated until they ended up on
the West Coast of Africa. As predicted by The Lord,
Jerusalem was overthrown, the Temple was destroyed,
and the Black negroes (Hebrew/Israel people) were
scattered (See Matt. 24:15-21; Luke 21: 5-6, 20-24).
The loss of life was appalling, and so many of Israel's
people were slain that the whole lake of Galilee was
red with blood and covered with corpses. The noted
historian Josephus estimated that one million one
hundred thousand perished in the siege of Jerusalem.
The book, *The Jewish War of Flavius Josephus*
describes this massive genocide. In 70 A.D., Rome
brought a temporary end to the Nation of Israel.

God did not want the Israelites worshipping any

graven images or symbols. A cross, stone, box, or star is not needed to obtain salvation and acceptance into the Kingdom of God. These are all ideas from the rulers of these other nations. The religion of Islam and Catholicism would not be in Africa today if it were not for the slave trade. These religions were initially brought on Blacks by force during their captivity. They learned to pray to the cross, which is made of wood. The Blacks (now Muslims) learned how to pray to the "Dome of the Rock" and the "Black Stone" or Kaaba in Mecca.

5. A Very Sick and Disease-Stricken People

The LORD will afflict you with all the diseases of Egypt that you feared so much, and you will have no relief.

Deuteronomy 28:60

No other race has experienced as much loss of life from slavery, famine, war, poverty, disease, or mass executions as Blacks. An increasing number of Blacks are diagnosed with mental illnesses (i.e., paranoid, schizophrenia, bipolar, depression, psychosis, and so on). Suicidal rates, alcoholism, drug use, crime, and high school dropouts for Blacks have also risen. This is now happening with Blacks more than any other race of people in America. Furthermore, Black Americans and Africans make up most of all HIV cases globally compared to any other race. Also, Black Americans are more likely to get hypertension, high cholesterol, diabetes, renal failure, morbid obesity, and coronary artery disease, among many other diseases. The Tuskegee Experiment was conducted because Whites believed syphilis behaved differently in Blacks, and supposedly, those with deeper African roots were, in some ways, immune to the disease. Nevertheless, black patients are still the subjects of this same type of experimentation today, except nowadays, it can be found in *medical training* and *clinical trials*.

Before the arrival of the Europeans, the Americas had been isolated from Europe and Africa. Contact with the Europeans brought measles and smallpox to the Native Indians (who were of the 10 Northern Tribes of Israel). In addition, numerous other diseases were brought to the Americas, such as scarlet fever, typhoid, typhus, influenza, pertussis, tuberculosis, cholera, diphtheria, chickenpox, sexually transmitted diseases, and measles. Many sources state that 25-50% of the Native tribes died from disease.

The Taino genocide (1492-1518) is when the Spanish wiped out most of the Tainos (Arawaks), the native people of the Caribbean Islands (present-day Cuba, Jamaica, Haiti, Dominican Republic, Puerto Rico, Bahamas, etc.). According to one estimate, genocide and disease wiped out 3 million of the 3.5 million Tainos (85%). Most were already dead when smallpox arrived in 1518. They were enslaved to do harsh work for the Spaniards; they were raped and brutally killed by the sword, guns, or man-eating dogs. Many of the Taino men of Puerto Rico, or "La Tiana," were killed in battle, disease, or suicide during the invasion of the Spanish Conquistadors. This, of course, left the Taino women on the island for intermarriage and mixing the white bloodline into the Taino bloodline.

6. At the Bottom with All Races Above You

The foreigners living among you will become stronger and stronger, while you become weaker and weaker. They will lend money to you, but you will not lend to them. They will be the head, and you will be the tail.

Deuteronomy 28:43-44

After the war, institutional injustices focused on stealing Blacks' land and jobs and ensuring African Americans did not build wealth as fast as the rest of Americans. Today's economy was built on this. Blacks borrow money from every other race and primarily work for every other race. Because we don't own anything, we are always subject to working for others who, in most cases, are not our people. Also, because we have no capital, we must rely on borrowing money from financial institutions owned by non-Black races. We borrow money from other races in the forms of high-interest loans, credit cards, pawn shops, and payday loan advances because we have no money to lend to each other.

After desegregation, Blacks started to lose their businesses because of the competition they faced with other non-Black businesses in white America. No longer did Blacks depend on each other; desegregation allowed them to spend their money with any race anywhere in America, which is exactly what they did, just like today. The integration of Blacks into white America gave them a chance to work for other races other than their own, giving them a false sense of success in America. In New York, waves of immigrants (Jews, Italians, Greeks, Asians, Middle Eastern, Indians, and Latinos) started to flood America, setting up businesses that are still thriving today. Blacks became their employees, not reaping any benefits whatsoever.

In today's world, 400 years after slavery, despite America being built with the blood of our forefathers, we, as Blacks, continue to work for other races and give our money away to other races. This, in turn, ensures the success of those races, not ours. It is known that there are more Asian restaurants in America than fast food restaurants. Many local Arab grocery stores, liquor stores, corner stores, and gas stations are stocked with food purchased with government EBT (Electronic Benefits Transfer cards), food assistance cards, or special government-supplied credit cards.

Because the Arabs and Chaldeans do not use their money to buy their store stock products but instead use the government's money, the profits they receive from Blacks buying these goods, using their money or EBT/Food Assistance money, is over 100%. All the businesses in the black community are designed to take our money. Unfortunately, this does nothing for us; instead, it allows the children of these other races to have easier roads to success so that they will be our children's future bosses. America, post-slavery, devised different strategies and plans to reduce the population of African Americans while increasing other immigrant races. No matter where Blacks live, there is always another race making money off the land and the people that live within it. Blacks have been in America for over 400 years, longer than every other immigrant race, yet we don't own anything, and we provide the labor workforce for all these other races.

Daily, we watch the Jewish-controlled media as they push their agenda to exploit and display negative and destructive images via television shows and the news. The racism, discrimination, and treatment Blacks received from other races simply because of the color of our skin do not happen to any other race of people.

7. Stripped of Identity, Culture, and Religion

You will become an object of horror, ridicule, and mockery among all the nations to which the LORD sends you.

Deuteronomy 28:37

The LORD will exile you and your king to a nation unknown to you and your ancestors. There in exile you will worship gods of wood and stone.

Deuteronomy 28:36

Once the evil European slave traders had Judah in their sights, they planned to bring them to the New World, the United States. Native Americans, also from the tribe of Israel, were being slaughtered by European invaders over their land. After causing the death of MILLIONS of Hebrews during their transport to America, Europeans began the systemic destruction of Israel as a nation. When the older slaves died, our entire heritage was lost. From then on, we were taught a new identity crafted by our European or Arab slave masters, from the food we were to eat to the White, blue-eyed Jesus and White Jews they made us believe was the truth.

- Hebrew names were changed to European names.
- Hebrews were forced to speak English and forbidden to speak Hebrew.
- Hebrews were forbidden to read the Bible and were only allowed to teach what Europeans taught them.
- Hebrew families were split up and sold to different slave owners.
- Hebrew women were raped, and so were the men in an evil homosexual practice called

"buck breaking."
- Hebrew babies were used as bait to catch alligators and sometimes for sport.

Blacks and Latinos have adopted the religions of their slave masters in every country they have been scattered into. After the fall of Jerusalem in 70AD, the Catholic Church infused its man-made doctrines and white lies into Christianity because everything from the Bible was visually shown to us (the whitewashing of Jesus and the Bible) or taught to us orally.

The Israelites adopted Islam and then began praying to the BLACK STONE at Mecca (Saudi Arabia), placed on the eastern cornerstone of the 43-foot STONE CUBE building called the "Kaaba." Almost a millennium later, our people were introduced to European White-inspired Christianity with the complete Holy Bible (Old Testament/New Testament) modified by the Catholic Church. European Christianity brought the teachings of worshipping on Sunday, using the WOODEN CROSS as the symbol of Christianity and believing in the image of a white man with blue eyes as the Messiah (Christ).

8. Packed into Prisons and Jails

You will serve your enemies whom the LORD will send against you. You will be left hungry, thirsty, naked, and lacking in everything. The LORD will put an iron yoke on your neck, oppressing you harshly until he has destroyed you.

Deuteronomy 28:48

Our people as slaves worked in gruesome conditions in which they were in *starvation* and literal *nakedness*. Black slaves worldwide were shackled in chains, NAKED with an iron yoke around their necks and shackles on their hands and feet. Sometimes, Black slaves were attached to heavy pieces of wood or attached with chains to other slaves so that groups of slaves could not run away. This did not happen to the European Jews during the Holocaust or any other race other than Blacks. No other race of people has been rounded up to be sold as slaves in America and other countries to the magnitude that the black race has throughout history.

The lie that the 13th Amendment freed Hebrews has blinded most people to the fact that the American prison system is nothing more than slavery re-branded as *mass incarceration*. Eventually, this will all come to an end. If we do the math on how long Blacks have been enslaved in America, including the current prison system, the number will be astronomical.

In 1887, an investigation by a grand jury in Hinds

County, Mississippi, found that the prisoners in the state's convict leasing system were worked to death, kept in filthy conditions, and starved.

Private prison systems rack in approximately $1.7 billion a year. The United States has incarcerated more people than any other country globally, 85% being black men and women. Using the government as their puppet, the powerful elites conspired to make music that promoted criminal behavior to get the prisons filled. They used Black artists to promote gang-banging music (bait) that they had written, anticipating young consumers as the prey.

Policing in the U.S. has always been bound up with the color line. In the South, police departments emerged out of the 18th-century slave patrols—bands of men working to discipline slaves, facilitate their transfer between plantations, and catch runaways. In the North, the professional police department came about as a response to a series of mid-19th century urban upheavals, many of which, like the 1834 New York anti-abolition riot, had their origins in racial strife. Apparently, both came about to restrain Black people.

9. Merciless Death

Your corpses will be food for all the scavenging birds and wild animals, and no one will be there to chase them away.

Deuteronomy 28:26

During the massacre of the Native Americans, the Europeans attacked the towns and did not spare the children, the aged, pregnant women, or women in childbirth. They had not only stabbed them but dismembered them by cutting them to pieces as if dealing with sheep in a slaughterhouse. They laid bets as to who, with one stroke of the sword, could split a man in two, cut off his head, or spill out his entrails with a single stroke of the pike. They cut open the belly of pregnant women, allowing their babies to fall to the dogs. They took infants from their mother's breasts, snatching them by the legs and pitching them headfirst against the rock or throwing them into the river, roaring with laughter and saying as the babies fell into the water, "Boil there, you offspring of the devil."

The eating of human flesh by animals and birds happened regularly for black slaves after lynchings and other ruthless killings. It was reported that out of 10 million slaves sold each year, 9 million black slaves died from the harsh conditions of slavery even before making it to their destination. During the slave trade, slave ships were frequently followed by sharks waiting for food, and slave caravans were frequently followed by scavenger birds or hyenas ready for an easy meal.

Blacks were linked two by two and driven through the medieval forests to the coast. These painful treks required weeks; some frequently became ill and felled by exhaustion. Many were unable to rise even though the bull whip was applied as an encourager. They were left to die and were devoured by wild beasts. It was not unusual to see the bones of the dead lying in the tropical sun, a sad and gruesome reminder to those who would later tread this path.

10. Restless and Without Peace

You will grope around in broad daylight like a blind person groping in the darkness, but you will not find your way. You will be oppressed and robbed continually, and no one will come to save you. You will suffer under constant oppression and harsh treatment. You will go mad because of all the tragedy you see around you.

Deuteronomy 28:29; 33-34

There among those nations you will find no peace or place to rest.

Deuteronomy 28:65

Once on the slave ship, the next step was to shave the hair from the head of the acquired slaves. Then they were bound and branded with a hot iron, either on the back, or the hip, identifying them with their owners. Now the Negro slave was indeed the property of the Jewish purchaser. If he fled, he could be identified. After this process, there was a farewell celebration. There were instances when entire families were brought out of the interior to the coast and separated through the buyer—the father going with one ship and sons and daughters another. These *farewell* celebrations were usually packed with emotion, tears, drama, and sadness. There was little joy, if ever.

Slaves spent most of their time on their hands, knees, and feet doing slave work. We could only imagine the sores they received and the pain they experienced while forced to do slave labor for countless hours in the harsh elements. Slaves did not get sick leave or short-term disability to ease their wounds, sores, or aching bones; they endured the physical pain of working in the hot fields and the pain of being continuously beaten with bullwhips by the slave masters.

Being *Black* in America, for parents and children, is full of constant worry— worrying if dad will make it home safe, worrying that our Black sons and daughters are not the victims of Black-on-Black crime, hate crimes, or police brutality/a judicial system that puts a target on Blacks and labels us as *the problem*. We are constantly under surveillance. We are the most monitored, controlled, photographed, and spied upon race.

No matter what country Blacks live in, it seems they are strategically suppressed by the evil powers to be in that land or country. In America, despite supposedly living in "the land of the free," where "all men are created equal," Blacks walk around every day still not feeling totally free. We have been conditioned to *fit in* with everyone else instead of being able to be ourselves without discrimination.

11. Families Split, No History, Legacy, or Ownership

You will be engaged to a woman, but another man will sleep with her. You will build a house, but someone else will live in it. You will plant a vineyard, but you will never enjoy its fruit. You will watch as your sons and daughters are taken as slaves. Your heart will break for them, but you won't be able to help them.

Deuteronomy 28:30; 32

Slavery broke up families as children were enslaved as well. It was common in slavery to see young boys taken from their fathers and young girls separated from their mothers only to be sold to a sexually abusive slave master.

In the mid-1500s, the European Spaniards separated men and women so they could not have sex. The Spaniards chose the native women they wanted to have sex with and those they wanted to forcefully marry, bearing mulatto children. Over time, millions of native people died, the men dying in the mines and the women dying in the field from exhaustion or hunger. This is how they depopulated the land of the natives and got rich.

It is a known fact that our black women in America were raped by their slave masters and their slave master's friends. The slave masters had no regard for raping the younger or older female slaves. It was a common practice to break families up during the slave auctions. All races can sleep with a black woman for sexual desires, but when their women are involved with black men, it is forbidden, taboo, and a disgrace to their family. During the Arab slave trade, to ensure that the Black male slaves would not impregnate Arab women, Arab slave traders castrated the black males (cut their penises and testicles).

During the transatlantic slave trade, white men exerted their power over the slaves even though they were easily outnumbered by them. If they wanted sex, they could take a slave and have sex with her, young, old, married, or unmarried. If young white boys wanted sex, it was also available to them, male or female. If they wanted to see men and women having sex, they could set it up. If they wanted to have sex orgy parties using Black slaves with all their friends, they easily could have done so. Likewise, some single white women purchased black male slaves just for sex, despite the backlash. This sexual control they had over the slaves corrupted the South and, at the same time, broke many black families apart. It mentally scarred and destroyed Blacks for generations.

12. Controlling Laws

Your life will constantly hand in the balance. You will live night and day in fear, unsure if you will survive. In the morning you will say, 'If only it were night.' And in the evening you will say, 'If only it were morning.' For you will be terrified by the awful horrors you see around you.

Deuteronomy 28:66-67

Laws were established to criminalize what we, as Blacks, normally practice or do. Vagrancy laws allowed police to sweep up black men and rent them out for convict labor. Following the war, convict leasing programs shifted the southern prison populations to predominantly black.

Black codes in the antebellum South regulated the activities and behavior of Blacks, especially free Blacks, who were not considered citizens. Chattel slaves lived under the complete control of their owners, so there was little need for extensive legislation. All Southern states imposed at least minimal limits on slave punishment, for example, by not making murder or life-threatening injury of slaves a crime, and a few states allowed slaves a limited right of self-defense. As slaves, they could not use the courts or sheriff or give testimony against a white man. North Carolina restricted slaves from leaving their plantations. If a male slave tried to court (date) a female slave on another property, he needed a pass to pursue this relationship. Without this pass, he would risk severe punishment at the hands of the patrollers.

Jim Crow laws were state and local laws that enforced racial segregation in the southern United States. The laws were enacted in the late 19th and early 20th centuries by white southern Democrat-dominated state legislatures to disenfranchise and remove political and economic gains made by Blacks during the Reconstruction Period. The Jim Crow laws were enforced until 1965 and mandated racial segregation in all public facilities in the former confederate states of America and some others, beginning in 1870. As a body of law, Jim Crow stated that constitutional provisions mandated the segregation of public schools, public places, public transportation, restrooms, restaurants, and drinking fountains between Blacks and Whites.

- In 1740, South Carolina enacted the Negro Act, allowing slave masters to whip and kill slaves who violated the law by growing their food, learning to read, assembling in groups, or earning money.
- In 1804, Virginia's legislature passed a law outlawing all nighttime meetings of enslaved people, such as unlawful assemblies. The crime was made punishable by up to 20 lashes.
- In 1829, Cincinnati, Ohio, invoked a law to force black residents to leave the city.

- In 1844, after slavery was declared illegal in Oregon, the state passed a law prohibiting black people from residing in the state and authorizing the whipping of black people yet found in the state.
- In 1865, Mississippi made it a crime punishable by fines and imprisonment for free black adults to be unemployed or to assemble.
- In 1875, Tennessee passed laws authorizing racial discrimination in hotels, public transportation, and places of amusement.

Today slavery has been made 100% legal if it's a punishment for a crime. According to the 13th Amendment of the U.S. Constitution: *"Neither slavery nor involuntary servitude, except as a punishment for crime whereof the party shall have been duly convicted, shall exist within the United States, or any place subject to their jurisdiction."* However, ever since slavery became privatized to the prison industry, laws have been made to specifically target people of color to put them back into slavery.

After reading the curses of Deuteronomy, how can anyone deny that these curses directly reflect the plight of Blacks? This proves without a shadow of a doubt that those of us who have been scattered via slavery are the true descendants of the Ancient Hebrew Israelites mentioned in the Bible.

NOTES

CHAPTER THREE

BIBLICAL HISTORY OF "I CAN'T BREATHE"

In this chapter, we will continue to unfold why so many people, specifically Blacks, find themselves in dire circumstances in which they are at the mercy of another, crying out, *"I can't breathe."* Let us begin by taking a look at the different nations the Most High allowed to take the children of Israel captive due to our ancestors' disobedience and the continued disobedience of the true children of Israel (Blacks) today.

Egypt

Our story in Egypt begins with Joseph, who was one of the twelve sons of our forefather, Jacob, (whose name was changed to Israel). At a young age, Joseph was sold into Egyptian slavery by his jealous brothers. After gaining favor with God and Potiphar (captain of Pharaoh's guard). Potiphar, in time, recognized

Joseph's gifts, talents, and trustworthiness and made him steward over his entire estate. After interpreting the Pharoah's dream, Joseph was appointed as overseer of the entire kingdom. During the seven years of famine, Joseph's entire family came to Egypt and was given the land of Goshen. Now Joseph and his brothers and all their generation died, and the Israelites had been in Egypt for generations; they multiplied and significantly increased in numbers.

Then the new Pharaoh, who did not know Joseph, saw that the Israelites had become so numerous that he feared their presence. He feared that if war broke out, they would join with the enemy and fight against the Egyptians. Gradually and stealthily, he forced them to become his slaves to kill their spirits and stop their growth. *Doesn't this sound familiar? Has not the spirit of the Black community been killed? Has not our economic growth become stagnant?* The Israelites were oppressed by forced labor. Some slaves worked long hours in mud pits, while others were skilled carpenters, jewelers, and craftsmen. Regardless of their skill, all slaves were watched closely by brutal slave masters, supervisors whose assignment was to keep them working as fast as possible. They were specialists in making a slave's life miserable. They also made the slaves build grand treasure cities.

Pharoah, still worried that the Israelite slaves would rise against him, ordered a terrible punishment – *all the first-born male babies of the Israelites were to be killed. (Now, our babies are killed by planned parenthood. Black women have the highest abortion rate in the U.S.)* Pharaoh gave orders to the midwives that as they were helping the Israelite women during childbirth on the delivery stool, if they saw that the baby was a boy, they should kill him. The midwives, however, feared God and did not do what the King of Egypt had told them to do. Then, Pharaoh gave another order to all his people: *"Every Israelite boy that is born you must throw into the Nile but let every girl live."* As Pharaoh continued to oppress the children of God, they began crying out, *"I can't breathe."* God heard the cry of the people and brought many plagues upon the Egyptians, delivered His people from the Egyptians, and made all the Egyptians give up their wealth to the Israelites.

This was the first and only time the Israelites were *not* enslaved due to disobedience.

Assyria

In 721 B.C., Assyria swept out of the north, captured the Northern Kingdom of Israel, and took the ten tribes into captivity. From there, they became lost to history.

The warlike Assyrians became the dominant power in the Middle East late in the 9th century through the 7th century B.C. Their prominent rulers include Tiglath-pileser and Sargon II the Great, who carried Israel into captivity.

The Assyrians treated captives with cruelty. They tortured prisoners for entertainment by blinding them, cutting them, or pulling off strips of skin until they died. If the Assyrians wished to enslave a captive, they would often put a hook in his nose.

The sins of Israel's people caught up with them, and God allowed Assyria to defeat and disperse the people. They were led into captivity and swallowed up by the mighty, evil Assyrian empire. After the Israelites (Northern Kingdom) were deported, foreigners from the Assyrian empire were sent to resettle in the land. *The Northern Kingdom was deported to the Americas (the native so-called Indians).*

Israel was invaded by the Assyrians three times. Of course, the cry, *"I can't breathe,"* caused The Most High to demonstrate his mercy in the face of deserved judgment by giving the people repeated opportunities to repent.

Although Assyria did not know it was part of God's plan, God used this nation to judge his people. God accomplished His plans in history despite people or nations who rejected Him. Our all-powerful, sovereign God is still in control today. Therefore, we have security, even in a rapidly-changing world. Because our people of Samaria and Jerusalem (the Northern Kingdom) were worshiping idols and other gods, God allowed Assyria to overtake them.

Daniel prophesied the Gentile's world power that would reign over God's people because of their disobedience, being in a constant state of "I can't breathe." This is called the times of the Gentiles (Luke 21:24).

Babylonian/Chaldeans (Head Made of Gold- Daniel Prophecy

According to the Zondervan Illustrated Bible Dictionary, Babylon was a powerful nation centered between the Tigris and Euphrates rivers in modern Iraq. This nation succeeded the Assyrians in dominating the Middle East under kings Merodach-baladan, Nabopolassar, and Nebuchadnezzar.

In II Chronicles 36, God's anger flared against His rebellious people. Therefore, He allowed Babylon to conquer Assyria and become the new world power. The Babylonian army marched into Jerusalem, burned the temple, tore down the city's massive walls, and carried off the people into captivity.

After watching their brothers and sisters (the Northern Kingdom) go into exile, Judah (the Southern Kingdom) continued in sin. God allowed them to be defeated by the Babylonians, who exiled many of them, but they were not (at this time) scattered, and their land (at this time) was not repopulated. Sometimes we do not learn from the examples of sin and foolishness around us.

The Babylonian policy for taking captives differed from that of the Assyrians, who moved most of the people out and resettled the land with foreigners. Instead, the Babylonians took only the strong and skilled, leaving the poor and weak to rule the land, thus elevating them to positions of authority and winning their loyalty.

Judah was invaded by the Babylonians three times. Again, the cry, "I can't breathe," demonstrated God's mercy for Judah. But continued disobedience forced God to relent and allow them to go into captivity.

Medo-Persian (Chest and Arm of Silver - Daniel's Prophecy)

Again, because of the children of Israel's disobedience, the Most High allowed them to be taken captive by the Medo-Persian. Persia, modern Iran, succeeding the Babylonian kingdom in the mid-sixth century B.C., was the major political force in the Middle East. The Medo-Persian empire included the lands of Media and Persia. Many Persian kings— Cyrus the Great, unified and ruled over the Medes and Persians for over 30 years, establishing the largest empire the world had yet seen. Cyrus overran the crumbling empire of the Babylonians. He encouraged religious tolerance. This policy was extended to the people of God who had been enslaved and had suffered religious repression by the Babylonians. King Darius, the Mede, acquired the kingdom of Babylon when king Belshazzar was slain, and that empire fell to the Medes and Persians. Also, Artaxerxes played a role in the history of the Israelites, returning them to their homeland to end the Babylon Exile.

The Most High used Cyrus to fulfill certain prophecies of Jeremiah and Isaiah regarding the liberation of the Israelites from Babylonian captivity and rebuilding the temple in Jerusalem.

Zerubbabel, Ezra, and Nehemiah were allowed to return to Jerusalem to rebuild the temple, help the people with their spiritual needs, and rebuild the city walls.

Greece (Belly and Thighs of Bronze - Daniel's Prophecy)

The Most High, *being our Omniscient God*, allowed the Greek to defeat the Medo-Persians, whereby the Israelites were in captivity under Greece. Alexander the Great ruled from 336-323 B.C. (1 Maccabees 1:1). He was the son of King Philip II and educated by the Greek philosopher Aristotle to have a passion for learning and an unshakable belief in the superiority of Greek (Hellenistic) culture. Alexander attacked the Medo-Persian to free Greeks living under their thumb in Asia Minor. After several victories, Hellenistic was the international norm for civilization. He took Persians into his army, encouraged his soldiers to marry Asians, and began to establish Greek cities in the East; many named Alexandria. Alexander's shrewd genius, visionary leadership, and outstanding military command helped him accomplish his ambitions. He died in Babylon at the young age of 32. His vast empire was divided among his four generals. Ptolemies controlled Egypt and Israel, and Seleucids controlled Persia, Syria (Palestine), and Asia Minor—these two reigned. Israel lay between these two nations, thus being used as a battleground—wasting the land and killing the people. His other two generals were Cassander and Lysimachus. Alexander's legacy eventually contributed to the rise of the Roman Empire and the spread of Christianity.

Greek became the language of literature and commerce throughout the "inhabited world," hence the New Testament being written in Greek.

Rome (Legs of Iron - Daniel's Prophecy)

The fourth and last nation the Most High allowed to take the children of Israel into captivity was Rome.

The fourth beast shall be the fourth kingdom upon the earth, which shall be diverse from all the whole earth, and shall tread it down, and break it in pieces.
Daniel 7:23

Rome remains a nation today, for Rome separated into ten European nations (Great Britain, Spain, Germany, France, Belgium, Netherlands, Luxemburg, Denmark, Switzerland, and Sweden) and is symbolic of America today.

The ten horns of the beast are ten kings who have not yet risen to power. They will be appointed to their kingdoms for one brief moment to reign with the beast.

Revelation 17:12

The laws of western civilization is from ancient Rome. It is spoken of in the Book of Daniel as the little horn, which incorporated the three powers of Europe: Great Britain, France and Spain.

I considered the horns, and behold, there came up among them another little horn, before whom there were three of the first horns plucked up by the roots.

Daniel 7:8

Antiochus III, the Seleucid Dynasty—greedy to conquer, never satisfied—invaded Greece. Antiochus was totally defeated in a series of encounters with the Roman commander Scipio.

During the New Testament times, the Romans controlled most of the known world around the Mediterranean, including Judea. Their vast empire spread, and the Romans merged elements of various religions into their own pantheon of gods, including Greek mythology (which is not mythology at all) and several eastern cults. Like Babylon, in the Old Testament, the Roman Empire became a New Testament symbol of paganism, idolatry, and oppression. Eventually, Rome adopted a policy of brutal persecution against the church, which, at that time, were Israelites. Christianity eventually became the dominant religion of the Roman Empire under Emperor Constantine. Rome was the capital of the "Gentile world."

The Catholic Church pretends to be a true church, but it is based on the Babylonian Mystery religion. Revelation 17:5, And on her forehead (the Catholic Church) a name was written:

"MYSTERY BABYLON THE GREAT
THE MOTHER OF HARLOT AND THE
ABOMINATIONS OF THE EARTH."

They are called "Mystery Babylon the Great" because they pretend to be Christian, but they are really the Babylonian religion of Sun and Satan worship.

In 1564 A.D., Pope Pius IV proclaimed, in the Council of Trent, 12 decrees which he charged all men that would be saved to own and to swear unto. The 11th one states: "I do acknowledge that the holy Catholic and apostolic Roman Church to be the mother and mistress of all churches: And I do promise to swear true allegiance to the Bishop of Rome, the successor of St. Peter, the prince of the apostles, and Vicar of Jesus Christ.

The Catechism of the Catholic Church proclaims
that they are the 'Mother,' the author of salvation,
the teacher in the faith, and the head of all believers,
which is an abomination.

Revelation 17:4 says," And the woman was arrayed in purple and scarlet colour and decked with gold and precious stones and pearls." The color for the Catholic Church's Bishops and other prelates is purple and scarlet for cardinals. The papal church is adorned with gold, precious stones, and pearls. In Revelation 17:5, John had been shown that the Babylonian pagan religion was still alive and would manifest itself in the form of the Harlot Church. Roman Catholicism is really the pagan Babylonian religion of Sun and Satan worship, mysteriously masked by the cover of Christianity. The influence of the Pope is everywhere, as priests and Catholic Churches are in most countries of the world.

Rome (whose rulers are the Pope and the wealthy Elites) reigns over the earth. The Jesuits control the city-state of Vatican City, which controls the world's religious and political leaders. They control the city of London, the world's financial power, and the city-state of Washington D.C., the world's military power. Rome has hidden by dividing into the European nations, including its daughter, "America." Rome is yet ruling.

In 1773, Mayer Amschel Rothschild assembled twelve of his most influential friends and convinced them that if they all pooled their resources together, they could rule the world. This meeting took place in Frankfurt, Germany. Adam Weishaupt was appointed to lead this effort. May 1, 1776, Weishaupt established a secret society called the Order of the Illuminati. Weishaupt is the professor of Canon Law at the University of Ingolstadt in Bavaria, part of Germany. The Illuminati seek to establish a New World Order.

The insignia of the Order of the Illuminati first appeared on the reverse side of U.S. one-dollar bills in 1933. At the base of the 13-story pyramid, one can read the year 1776 (MDCCLXVI in Roman numerals). The eye radiating in all directions is the *all-spying eye* that symbolizes the terroristic, Gestapo-like agency set up by Weishaupt. The Latin words, *ANNUIT COEPTIS*, mean *our enterprise (conspiracy) has been crowned with success*. Below, *NOVUS ORDO SECLORUM* explains the nature of the enterprise: a *New Social Order* or a *New World Order*.

CHAPTER FOUR

SLAVERY IN AMERICA

In 70 A.D., Rome (which later became the European Nation) brought a temporary end to the Nation of Israel—burning the city of Jerusalem, bringing a great sword and slaughter. Roman hatred for God and vengeance on his people was so great that the Israelites, running from persecution, migrated until they ended up on the west coast of Africa. During the period from Pompey to Julius, it has been estimated that over 1,000,000 black Jews fled to Africa from Roman persecution and slavery (Luke 21: 20-24). The loss of life was appalling, and so many of our people were slain that the whole lake of Galilee was red with blood and covered with corpses. The noted historian Josephus estimated that one million one hundred thousand perished in the siege of Jerusalem.

NOTE *The Jewish War of Flavius Josephus describes this massive genocide.*

As I stated earlier, God wants to expose the lies embedded in the fabric of our society. Unfortunately, history is NOT as we have come to know it. European immigration to America had NOTHING to do with seeking *religious liberty.* The story of the slaves in America begins with Christopher Columbus, a Jew, who was accompanied by five 'Marranos' (Jews who had foresworn their religion and supposedly became Catholics), who sailed to the New World to seek out the Lost Tribe of Israel. They were sold on the idea of capturing 500 Indians and selling them as slaves in Seville, Spain. This, ironically, was the beginning of slavery in the Americas. The converted Jews were expelled from Spain on August 2, 1492, and Portugal in 1497. Many of these Jews emigrated to Holland, where they set up the Dutch West Indies Company to exploit the new world. In 1654, the first Jew, Jacob Barsimson, emigrated from Holland to New Amsterdam (New York). In the next decade, many more followed him, settling along the East Coast, principally in New Amsterdam and Newport, Rhode Island.

They were prevented by ordinances issued by Governor Peter Stuyvesant from engaging in the domestic economy, so they quickly discovered that the territory inhabited by the Indians would be a fertile field. No laws prevented the Jews from trading with the Indians. The first Jew to begin trading with the Indians was Hayman Levy, who was soon joined by Jews Nicholas Lowe and Joseph Simon. Lowe conceived the idea of trading rum and whiskey to the Indians and set up a distillery in Newport, where these two liquors were produced. Within a short time, there were 22 distilleries in Newport, all owned by Jews, manufacturing and distributing *firewater*. The story of the debauching of the Indians with its resultant massacres of the early settlers is dramatic. The early Thanksgiving holidays were the celebrations of successful racial massacres.

The Red Holocaust was systematic, calculated, and extremely profitable. Colonial merchants supplied the British, Dutch, French, and American armies to ethnically cleanse the Indian Nations (Black Israelites) from their ancestral lands. Once the armies retreated, those merchants (Jews) surveyed and divided the land into lots and began selling them to the white settlers.

It is essential to comprehend the seaport of Newport. It is also important to recognize the Jewish share in slave commerce. There was a period when it was commonly referred to as The Jewish Newport-World Center of Slave Commerce. Altogether, there were six Jewish communities in North America: Newport, Charleston, New York, Philadelphia, Richmond, and Savannah. Eventually, the European people joined the Jews in what would become the biggest crime of sex/human trafficking against humanity.

The slave markets were full of black Jewish slaves. The black Jews carried their culture, history, laws, and written records with them; this assured them a constant precedent for developing a higher social organization. The Jews made use of every opportunity; they were industrious and skillful people. Kings, princes, governors, generals, secretaries, treasurers, revenue agents, judges, architects, engineers, doctors, historians, language interpreters, mathematicians, jewelers, sculptors, masons, carpenters, painters of art, goldsmiths, leatherworkers, potters, armorers, saddlers, blacksmiths, and agriculturists were found in the Jewish Ghanaian states.

Everything in the Western world—its cities, institutions, and wealth—has been built on the profits of Black slavery. The true Israelites built America into one of the greatest nations on the planet. Paris, Rome, Amsterdam, Seville, Lisbon, London, New York; name the place, and its riches are the spoils of the greatest CRIMINAL ENDEAVOR in the history of the universe. The United States paid reparations to slaveholders, not to slaves. Harvard scholar David B. Wilkins wrote, "*Slavery set this nation on a path in which it was necessary to portray blacks as mentally, emotionally, and spiritually incapable of self-determination.*" America is a nation built on the back of slavery, racism, and white supremacy.

The United States is controlled and manipulated by a private foreign power, and our unlawful Federal

US Government is their pawnbroker. The United States was not founded on the Lord Jesus Christ, as we all have been led to believe. Yes, it was founded on God, but *whose and what god?* The premise that the United States was founded on Christianity is a mere smokescreen. Case in point: Who was the Declaration of Independence written to and for? *Certainly not Black people.* Did not the Founding Fathers of the United States own slaves? What is Christianity? According to Google, it is the religion based on the person and teachings of Jesus of Nazareth or its belief and practices. The Jesus of the Bible that I know does not advocate the dehumanized treatment of any individual; therefore, perceiving or insisting that the Founding Fathers were Christians is an oxymoron. On the contrary, they were all Freemasonry, the teachings and practices of the secret fraternal (men only) order of Free and Accepted Masons, the largest worldwide secret society, which has nothing in common with our Lord Jesus Christ. Moreover, Kurdish Arabs and the European Nations under the rulership of Rome (Vatican) have been enslaving the *Negroes* and so-called *Native Indians*—the real children of Israel—under the disguise of America being a Christian nation.

America was more than just evil. It was and still is a declaration of war against God and his chosen people. Joel 3 explains why the events in the book of Revelation will take place. It's all over the enslavement of Israel.

Proclaim ye this among the Gentiles; Prepare war, *wake up the mighty men, let all the men of war draw near; let them come up: Beat your plowshares into swords, and your pruninghooks into spears: let the weak say, I am strong.* **Assemble yourselves, and come, all ye heathen, and gather yourselves together round about: thither cause thy mighty ones to come down, O LORD.**

Joel 3:9-11

The Bible gives us the precise timeline of when the enslavement of Israel had to take place. It tells us all about the people that plotted to enslave Israel, where the Israelites would be taken, and how they would be taken there. There is so much overwhelming evidence that has been uncovered that anyone denying the facts is only doing so out of hatred for Blacks, ignorance of the subject, or a combination of both.

They made conscious choices to side with Satan and declared war on God and His people. This was only the beginning of the first groups of slaves brought to America. For almost 200 more years, Europeans would continue to kidnap, rape, torture, beat, murder, and scatter Judah.

CHAPTER FIVE

WHY WAS ISRAEL ENSLAVED?

Why was Israel enslaved? The enslavement of Israel happened for one reason. Israel rebelled against God and started worshiping false gods like the nations around them. It started after the Exodus with Aaron and continued throughout the Bible.

According to the Bible, Hebrews did not migrate anywhere. Instead, they were taken as slaves, scattered by force, and would be oppressed for 400 years in a land they didn't know. The following scriptures support this claim.

And I will scatter you among the heathen and will draw out a sword after you: and your land shall be desolate, and your cities waste.

Leviticus 26:33

And the LORD shall scatter you among the nations, and ye shall be left few in number among the heathen, whither the LORD shall lead you.

Deuteronomy 4:27

And the LORD shall scatter thee among all people, from the one end of the earth even unto the other; and there thou shalt serve other gods, which neither thou nor thy fathers have known, even wood and stone.

Deuteronomy 28:64

I said, I would scatter them into corners, I would make the remembrance of them to cease from among men.

Deuteronomy 32:26

For the LORD shall smite Israel, as a reed is shaken in the water, and he shall root up Israel out of this good land, which he gave to their fathers, and shall scatter them beyond the river, because they have made their groves, provoking the LORD to anger.

1 Kings 14:15

Remember, I beseech thee, the word that thou commanded thy servant Moses, saying, If ye transgress, I will scatter you abroad among the nations.

Nehemiah 1:8

And they shall fall by the edge of the sword and shall be led away captive into all nations: and Jerusalem shall be trodden down of the Gentiles, until the times of the Gentiles be fulfilled.

Luke 21:24

Be confident, my people, you who are the legacy of Israel! You weren't sold to the nations for complete destruction, but you were handed over to your opponents because you made God angry. You upset your Creator when you sacrificed to demons and not to God. You forgot the eternal God who raised you.

Baruch 4:5-8

In 70 A.D., Emperor Titus invaded Jerusalem and destroyed the temple. According to the book of Josephus, over 1.1 million Hebrews were killed during this invasion. We know for a fact that the Hebrews fled to Africa to escape.

The Nations knew that if we (THE HEBREW ISRAELITES) were in the midst of sin, God would punish us and give us into the hands of the other nations. They also knew that if we kept the commandments, God would defend us, and we will rule. Our slave masters took our Bible, our heritage, made it their own (paganism), and re-taught it to us in their way to keep us in a confused state of mind, which is where we are today; not knowing who we are and still in sin! This was the curse spoken of in Lamentations 5:2, Jeremiah 17:4, and Deuteronomy

28:48. God says in Amos 3:2, "You only have I known of all the families of the earth; therefore, I will punish you for all your iniquities."

Whatever we agree with is what we give legal permission to operate in our lives. When we agree with ungodly spirits and practices, a demonic atmosphere develops. Stop agreeing and accepting what doesn't belong to you.

At one time, you were like a dead person because of the things you did wrong and your offenses against God. You used to live like people of this world. You followed the rule of a destructive spiritual power. This is the spirit of disobedience to God's will that is now at work in persons whose lives are characterized by disobedience.

Ephesians 2:1-2

Our people are chasing everything under the sun except our Creator, The Most High God. Therefore, awakening our people to the truth MUST BE A PRIORITY for those who seek and know the truth.

WE WERE PUNISHED SEVERELY FOR NOT KEEPING THE COMMANDMENTS!

CHAPTER SIX

WHO IS THE TRUE NATION OF ISRAEL?

We, those who were brought from Africa to America on slave ships, are the true Israelites (Hebrews), the physical descendants of Abraham, Isaac, and Jacob, a treasured possession of the Most High. We were exiled from the land of Israel after the Romans destroyed the Second Temple in 70 AD.

Before the Renaissance Period, the world knew Christ and Hebrews were black. In addition, there was no debate about the ethnicity of Christ or Hebrews. The Europeans attempted to change history to make themselves comfortable by pushing lie after lie until the truth was too obscured to see clearly.

Hebrew slavery is prophesied in the Old and New Testaments. Hebrews were told they'd be scattered around the world via slavery. They were also told that the final slavery would be via slave ships across the ocean. The topic of slavery in connection with

Bible prophecy is avoided because those currently claiming to be Jews in Israel cannot prove they were scattered around the world via slave ships. In fact, they don't have any history of slavery at all because they are European imposters. They simply don't fit the prophecies; therefore, focusing on a prophetic sign that doesn't fit them will expose the truth. No other nations of people can relate to the prophecy in Deuteronomy 28:15-68, but Black people and those of us scattered among other nations.

12 Tribes of Israel

JUDAH	American Blacks
BENJAMIN	West Indian Blacks /Jamaicans
LEVI	Haitians
EPHRAIM	Puerto Ricans
MANASSEH	Cubans
SIMEON	Dominicans
ZEBULON	Guatemala to Panama/ Columbia
GAD	Native North American Indians
REUBEN	Seminole Indians
ASHER	Columbia/ Brazil/ Argentina
ISSACHAR	Mexicans (Aztecs)
NAPHTALI	Chile /Hawaiians/ Samoans

CHAPTER SEVEN

WHO ARE THE JEWS IN ISRAEL?

I f Blacks are the chosen people of God, then who are those Jews over in Israel? They are imposters. They have assassinated our character and stolen our identity.

In the book of Genesis, Isaac and his wife Rebekah gave birth to twin boys. Esau, who came out first, was the ancestor of the Edomites, and Jacob, whose name was later changed to Israel, was the ancestor of the Israelites. The Most High told Rebekah that the elder should serve the youngest. That prophecy has not yet come to pass. Esau's descendants are the ruling class today. These are the Elite Jewish people and other Europeans. We know that our God cannot lie; therefore, Jacob's descendants, the true Children of Israel, will rule when Christ returns.

During the Maccabees revolt and victory, John Hyrcanus I forced Judaism's conversion on the Edomites (Idumea), Esau's ancestors who evolved the European Nations. They were told to *either convert or leave their country.* Anyone who embraced Judaism was called a *Jew.* In the Bible, while Rome was in control, Jesus identified these converts as the Pharisees and Sadducees. Jesus was NOT a Jew; neither were the disciples nor the 12 Tribes of Israel because they did not embrace Judaism. This is proof that the people called *Jews* at that time were simply Judaism converts from other nations like Greece, Syria, Edom, and Rome. There were also those called Ashkenazi Jews. The origin of the Ashkenazi Jews, who come most recently from Europe, has largely been shrouded in mystery. European Ashkenazi Jews are descended from the ancient people called the *Khazars.*

During the time after Attila the Hun's (ruled over the area known now as Russia, Eastern Europe, and Western Europe) death in the 7th Century (642 A.D.), the Arabs attempted to take control of Russia and Eastern Europe but were unsuccessful because of a powerful pagan empire called the *Khazarian Empire.* In 740 A.D., King Bulan, the first ruler of the Khazarian empire, adopted the religion of the Pharisees and Sadducees—Judaism. The Khazarian Kingdom converted its whole nation to Judaism.

NOTE *The true Children of Israel did not have to convert to Judaism to become God's Chosen People.*

The Khazars were a Turkish tribe who occupied the steps of Southern Russia, and Eastern Europe, all the way down to the Caucasus Mountains. The Caucasus Mountains are between the Black Sea on the left and the Caspian Sea on the right. So we get the name *Caucasians* from the Caucasus Mountains.

Originally, the Khazars spoke a Germanic-Slavic-Turkish language instead of Hebrew, which they would later combine with their language to form *Yiddish*. During this time, three major religions were being preached across Europe and the world: Islam, Christianity (established by the Roman Emperor Constantine), and Judaism (the religion/teaching of the Pharisees). King Bulan adopted Judaism as his Khazarian Kingdom's national religion. He had Jewish Rabbis teach his kingdom how to follow Judaism traditions and laws and learn the Hebrew alphabet and how to speak the language.

This was the official start of the European people called *Ashkenazi Jews*. The Ashkenazi Jews, thanks to the Jewish Rothschild Banking family, would later create the State of Israel after the Holocaust by way of the Balfour Declaration of 1917.

How is it that these Jews have propagated the idea that they are abused and persecuted people? To some degree, they have suffered some hardship throughout their history, which is also true for Blacks. The chief difference is that Jews were able to keep score. They made a tradition of persecution. No one has remembered the slaughter of thousands of Christians and the enslavement of Blacks in 50+ years, but the tragedy visited upon a few Jews is preserved forever in Jewish history. And they tell their woes not only to themselves but also to a sympathetic world.

I know the blasphemy of those who say they are Jews and are not, but are a synagogue of Satan.
Revelation 2:9 (written in red)

Behold, I will make them of the synagogue of Satan, which say they are Jews, and are not, but do lie; behold, I will make them to come and worship before thy feet, and to know that I have loved thee.
Revelation 3:9 (written in red)

And Jerusalem will be trampled down by the Gentiles, until the period of the Gentiles comes to an end.
Luke 21:24 (written in red)

NOTE *This means that only Gentiles should be in Jerusalem until the return of Christ when the Gentiles ruling the land will end.*

CHAPTER EIGHT

THE REAL ENEMY: SATAN

John 10:10 says, "The thief (Satan) cometh not but for to steal, and to kill, and to destroy."

STEAL *Our God, our name, our culture, our history, our land (Jerusalem), our truth (The Bible)*

KILL *plague – 1720; cholera – 1820; Spanish flu – 1920; Tuskegee syphilis – 1932; coronavirus – 2020*

DESTROY *Willie Lynch, Eugenics, The War on Drugs, mass incarceration*

In Ephesians 6:12, the Bible states, "For we are not fighting against flesh-and-blood enemies, but against evil rulers and authorities of the unseen world, against mighty powers in this dark world, against evil spirits in the heavenly places." *Who is the enemy?* He is an unemployed Cherub, a fallen angel. He is an invisible evil being. He is real. He does exist. He hates all humans. He is the Devil. His name is Satan. He was hurled out of Heaven for revolting against our Creator, The Most High God.

How art thou fallen from heaven, O Lucifer, son of the morning! ...For thou hast said in thine heart, I will ascend into heaven, I will exalt my throne above the stars ... I will be like the Most High.
Isaiah 14:12-14; Ezekiel 28:12-19

Because of his rebellion, Lucifer was mutated down to his present form of Satan, the ruler of darkness, and thrown out of heaven. Satan deceived Adam and Eve in the Garden of Eden by stealing the authority and dominion God had initially given to mankind. The Bible says in John 10:10, "The thief (Satan), does not come except to steal, and to kill and to destroy." Jesus came to give us back the Kingdom of God, our authority and dominion on the earth so that we may have life and not die twice.

Your adversary the devil, as a roaring lion, walketh about, seeking whom he may devour.
1 Peter 5:8

This great dragon—the ancient serpent called the devil, or Satan, the one deceiving the whole world— was thrown down to the earth with all his angels.
Revelation 12:9

So, the question is, **"How did the devil deceive the whole world?"** One of Satan's purposes on earth is to accuse you in your conscience. His greatest tool is deception because he has no real power (Colossians 2:15). He is the father of lies because this is what he feeds us, and lies are what we come to believe.

The Bible tells us that people perish for lack of knowledge. Thus, ignorance is man's number one problem. Satan has always depended upon an active body (his seed, the powerful elites) to execute and carry out those thoughts and lies that have been fed to us since childbirth. How has he carried out those lies? The media, public education, news, music, and movies influence our minds. Deception takes place first in the mind.

His active body has included the Rothschilds, Rockefellers, Oppenheimers, Bilderbergers, George Soros, Henry Kissinger, Bill Gates, and the Vatican; they all align themselves under the guise of "Freemasonry" (Illuminati/Secret Society). Their job is to create chaos in the world, thereby ushering in the New World Order (NWO). No one will enter the New World Order unless they pledge to worship Lucifer. For centuries, Satan has used his followers to devise a plan to deceive the whole world and take over planet Earth. Divide and conquer is the strategy of the elites. If they can keep the population divided, they can divide, conquer, and control. Let's take our eyes off who is in charge of this world and focus on who is in charge of our destiny, the One who says, *"The earth is mines and the fullness thereof and they that dwell therein.*" (Psalm 24:1-3). These powerful elites have conspired with the other nations to cut off the Most High God's Chosen People.

Psalm 83

God, don't be silent! Don't be quiet or sit still, God, because—look!—your enemies are in an uproar; those who hate you are acting arrogantly. They devise crafty schemes against your people; they plot against the people you favor, your precious ones. "Come on," they say, "let us wipe out Israel as a nation! We will destroy the very memory of its existence. Let the name Israel be remembered no more!

Psalm 83:1-4

Yes, this was their unanimous decision. They plotted with a single-minded heart. They signed a treaty as allies against God—and us, His people. These are the Edomites (European Nation) and Ishmaelites (Arab Nation); Moabites (Palestinians) and Hagrites; Gebalites, Ammonites (Jordanians), and Amalekites (The 13 Elite Jewish Families); and people from Philistia and Tyre. Assyria has joined them, too, and is allied with the descendants of Lot.

It was always the diabolical plan of the Nations, specifically the Amalekites and the European nations, in cahoots with Satan to strategically plan a slow kill for our people. As the days get closer to Christ's return, Satan and his minions are speeding up the process. Watch out, for this destruction is already upon us, so don't let it take you out!

NOTE *Amalek, Esau's grandson, was the son of his father's concubine. He was the ancestor of the wicked tribe known as the Amalekites, the first people to attack the Israelites on their way to The Promised Land.*

NOTES

CHAPTER NINE

THE VALLEY OF DRY BONES

T hen He asked, "Son of man, can these bones become living people again?" Then he said to me, "Speak a prophetic message to these bones and say, 'Dry bones, listen to the word of the LORD! This is what the Sovereign LORD says: Look! I am going to put breath into you, and you will come to life. Then you will know that I am the LORD."

Suddenly as I spoke, there was a rattling noise across the valley. The bones of each body came together and attached themselves as complete skeletons. Then as I watched, muscles and flesh formed over the bones. Then skin formed over the bones. Then skin formed to cover their bodies, but they still had no breath in them. Then he said to me, "Speak a prophetic message to the winds, son of man. Speak a prophetic message and say, 'This is what the Sovereign LORD says: Come, O breath, from the four winds! Breathe *into these dead bodies so they may live again." So, I spoke the message as He commanded me, and they all came to life and stood up on their feet—a great army, an extraordinary large company.*

He said to me, "Human one, these bones are the entire house of Israel, they represent the people of Israel. They are saying, 'We have said, 'Our bones are dried up, and our hope has perished...all hope is gone. Our nation is finished. Therefore, prophesy to them and say, 'This is what the Sovereign LORD says: O my people, I will open your graves of exile and cause you to rise again. Then I will bring you back to the land of Israel. When this happens, O my people, you will know that I am the LORD. I will put my Spirit in you, and you will live again and return home to your own land. Then you will know that I, the LORD, have spoken, and I have done what I said.

Ezekiel 37:3-14

This passage from Ezekiel is the current state of Blacks. We are spiritually dried up and desolate. Know that God has not forgotten about our plight. He is going to put a new song in our hearts. Those who put their trust in Him will soar high on wings like eagles. Do not give up, and do not give in; there has been a shift of favor. The Last shall be First.

What happened to the Hebrew Israelites that led them to be the people in the *Valley of Dry Bones*? The answer is found in Deuteronomy 28:1.

And it shall come to pass, if thou shalt hearken diligently unto the voice of the LORD thy God, to observe and to do all his commandants which I command thee this day, that the LORD thy God will set thee on high above all nations of the earth.

Deuteronomy 28:1

However, because we continue to be disobedient to God's laws and refuse to commit and obey Deuteronomy 28:1, we receive the curses: Deuteronomy 28:15 states, "But if it shall come to pass, if thou wilt not harken unto the voice of the LORD thy God, to observe to do all his commandants and his statutes which I command thee this day; that all these curses shall come upon thee, and overtake thee."

We are living in this scenario. Our people represent this *Valley of Dry Bones*, a miserable condition. A place of death and no hope. A situation that seems as if it will never change. But thanks to the God Almighty, in blessing us to "breathe" again, no longer will we cry out, "*I can't breathe.*" God told Ezekiel to prophesy to the dry bones so they could live. We, too, should be prophesying to the dry bones and one another so that we can live. We must break the control of this Beast System off of us. If we can't breathe, the enemy can keep us down. Rise and realize that you are the chosen people of God.

NOTES

CHAPTER TEN

UNDERSTANDING OUR ROLE IN CHRIST

As a young person growing up, I desired to please my parents. In our household, there were rules and laws that were beneficial for me to obey. My parents were the vehicle God used to bring me into the world. They provided for my health and welfare and ensured that I had food, shelter, clothing, and an education. They provided everything I needed to sustain life and taught me about life. I complied with the laws ordained by my parents, and because of that, I have lived a profitable life.

Notice, I said my parents were the vehicle used to bring me into the world, but God, the Creator of all things, literally created me and brought me into the world via my mother's womb. I was created in the Kingdom of Heaven. Genesis 1:27 states, "So God created man in His own image; in the image of God, He created him; male and female He created them."

The word *man* in Genesis 1:27 refers to mankind.

Therefore, you and I were created in the Kingdom of Heaven by an invisible God who is a Spirit. Because God (our Spiritual Father) is a Spirit (this is nothing spooky), He made us like him, a spirit. We look like God. We have His attributes. We have His character. Just as my parents were the vehicle to bring me to earth, I look like them; I have their attributes and character. Humans are spirits beings that have been given a soul (mind, will, and emotion) and clothed in an earth suit (our fleshly body) to live on earth.

I was obligated to obey my parents' laws (rules and guidance of the home). We understand that we are also obligated to obey men's laws. But we often disregard that we are obligated/commanded to obey God's laws. *Why did the Almighty God give us laws to obey?* Just as you give your children laws to obey and your country/ government gives laws to obey. At one point in society (especially in the United States), some of man's laws echoed God's laws, such as marriage (between male and female), abortions, sex, and adultery.

When we buy a car or an appliance, it comes with a user's operator manual. The first words on the manual are: Please read this manual carefully and thoroughly before operating. It goes on to give us a list of dangers/warnings, which are your *"dos and don'ts."* The manufacturer usually guarantees their product if it is used properly according to the manual. If you put water in your gas tank instead of gasoline, your car will not run. If you refuse to get an oil change, your vehicle's engine will start to have lots of problems. This can cause the engine to run less efficiently, and as time goes on, it will eventually cause the engine components to warp and wear out.

God is our manufacturer. The Bible is our user's manual. God has given us a list of danger/warnings, *"dos and don'ts."* We must read this manual (Bible) carefully and thoroughly before operating in life. When we fail to do so, not only will we not know the dos and don'ts, but we will also fail to operate properly in our daily lives.

The reason God put you on earth was to manage it. The word manage begins with man. It's the age when man is responsible for God's resources. To manage simply means to oversee another person's resources. God gave man dominion over the earth, which is management, and all humans are managers over God's property. God gave us rulership, not ownership. That means that in the Kingdom of God, no one owns anything. The earth is the Lord's and the fullness thereof and the world and they that dwell therein. No matter who claims to own whatever, God says, *"You are only a manager in my eyes, and I am watching how you handle my resources."* God will check to see if you can give an account of what He gave you. That includes relationships, money, investment, people, and opportunities.

Much of what we are taught in church is not

based on the Bible, but rather traditions gradually developed over the past 2000 years. These traditions have become so commonplace that few people question them or even think about questioning them.

Many Christian leaders would now tell us that we have no responsibility to the laws of God – that it's all about grace – that the law has been nailed to the cross. As a result, while most believers do not realize it, major components of contemporary Christianity violate the laws of our Creator. Christianity, as we know it, is a religion. The kingdom of God is not Christianity, nor is Christianity the Kingdom of God. Jesus never came to give us a religion but to give us back the Kingdom of God.

Let us address and correct one thing we all have been duped into believing. The Bible is NOT a religious book. It is not about religion. Religion can be explained as a set of beliefs concerning the universe's cause, nature, or purpose. In other words, religion is man's attempt to reconnect to Heaven through culture and traditions. Religion was not introduced or created by God. It is a deception of Satan. Why would the one and only Supreme God have many religions? The Bible is about establishing a government or the culture of Heaven in the earth. The Bible is a book about the Kingdom of Heaven and the Kingdom of God. The Kingdom of Heaven is a place or the invisible Kingdom, and the Kingdom of God is the culture of Heaven. God is the creator of heaven and earth. Genesis 1:1 states, "In the beginning God created the heaven and the earth." God decided that as the King of Heaven, He wanted to expand His territory to the earth. He also decided that He would extend His territory and establish the same authority and culture in Heaven, on the earth. Genesis 1:28 states," Fill the earth! Subdue it and have dominion over the fish of the sea and over the fowl of the air and over every living thing that moves upon the earth!"

What does the Kingdom of God look like? Matthew 6:33 states, "Seek the Kingdom of God above all else, and live righteously, and He will give you everything you need." The word *Kingdom* means the government of God. Seek God's government; seek God's way of doing things FIRST! His *righteousness*—that means right living, right standing; seek that FIRST, and all these other things you need and desire for life will be included. We have it backward; we are seeking all these other things FIRST. We should not seek after things but the One who can give us the things. Our Kingdom focus is to seek God's way of doing things (all day-everyday), which is His instructions in the Bible.

There is a way that seems right to man, but it ends in death.

Proverb 14:12

The Bible is a history book about a certain group of people that God chose to use to represent Him in the earth He created. Our mission was to establish the culture of Heaven on Earth. He established the entire human race through one man named Adam. God, the Father of Adam, explained to him the rules and laws of the household, and Adam complied. Adam had total authority and dominion over every living thing on the earth and communicated with an invisible God daily until one day, he did not follow the rules, and there were consequences.

God, the creator of Heaven, earth, and all mankind's sole purpose was to give man authority and dominion in the earth if they obeyed His rules and laws. To not die twice is about coming into the knowledge of this truth and transforming your ideology to line up with God's way of thinking–choosing to submit to His laws and not your own will or the deception of the enemy (Satan).

Did you know those who come into the Kingdom of God are Kings/Priests? The Bible tells us that Jesus has washed us from our sins with His blood and made us kings (Rev. 1:5-6), and as kings in Christ, our words carry power. In biblical times, a king's word carried tremendous power. What he decreed would come to pass. It was absolute. Watch what you say. Our words have power because they are a king's words. The devil is happy when you use the power of your words against yourself and your loved ones. He wants to see you defeated. Beloved, remember that as a king, what you say will come to pass because where the word of a king is, there is power. Learn to say what God says about you in His Word and watch His promises come to pass.

In times of uncertainty, destruction, and trouble, we need to pump ourselves up with God's word until we are full of the Spirit and have a consciousness of God. Do not feed on the negative words of man, the media, and Satan. If you are troubled, remember God is saying, *"Seek first my kingdom (My way of doing things: righteousness, peace, and joy in the Holy Spirit). Be conscious of the righteousness you have as a gift from My son (Jesus), and don't be conscious of your trouble. Keep your inner man flowing with My peace and joy, and I will take care of everything else."*

And when you come into the Kingdom, you can expect the glory of God to shine into every area of your life, including your family, job, and finances.

Once you receive Christ, you become a citizen of the Kingdom of Heaven and begin living as a kingdom citizen. As a citizen of Heaven, you have certain rights. We are citizens living in a spiritual Kingdom. In a democracy, supposedly, the majority rule; however, in a Kingdom, a king rules, and His rule is absolute. There is no debate with the king. When the king speaks, that settles it. Our king has made decrees. Every kingdom has decrees which are laws or rules we must obey. These rules are found in

the Bible (constitution). We live by the laws the king
has set forth, or we suffer His punishment or wrath.

CHAPTER ELEVEN

BREATHE AGAIN...

First, you must immediately begin to OBEY the laws, statutes, and commandments of OUR God. Secondly, you must realize that you are of the Lost Tribes of Israel. The Bible is our history book. It is about our God and our ancestors, Abraham, Isaac, and Jacob. You are of *royal blood*. You are NOT Africans. You are not a *byword*. You are not the descendants of slaves. The laws were given to us. Come out of sin! *What is sin?* Transgression, offense, or crime against God's laws. We are supposed to be the example for all the other nations to follow. Because the law was given to us, we are held accountable for our sin more than other nations. Other nations know the truth about us and understand that if we remain in sin, they will rule over us. Therefore, the other nations have conspired together in Psalm 83 to keep us in our deplorable sinful conditions. The very reason for the systemic racism and all laws criminalizing us. They portray us in the most degrading ways so that we can believe the worst about ourselves.

I was asked, "Why does it matter? Christ loves me anyway." Christ is coming back for a nation of people, not for individuals that He loves anyway. Understanding that we are the true Israelites is how we begin to be restored as a nation, and Satan and his people (those who are ruling) will begin to lose power. So, it DOES MATTER! Understand and have the revelation that you are Israel. We have to come out of this so-called Christianity that does not completely align with our Bible and begin to live for Christ according to the whole Bible and not only the New Testament. We cannot continue in sin because of grace—God forbid! Think about it; are we really obeying the Ten Commandments? Some may say yes. Think again! One commandment says, "Remember the Sabbath and keep it Holy." The Sabbath is the last day of the week. Did God change it to the first day of the week? Did grace change it, or did man change it? I submit to you that man (the Roman Catholic Church) changed it. We cannot truly serve Christ effectively when we do not know that we are the people of the Bible.

We must be aware of Satan's plans and strategy. Satan's deception in subliminal messages is everywhere, especially in music, movies, and Hollywood. We must be able to discern the signs and seasons of the times. There is a way that seems right to a man, but in the end is death. Everything you hear and see is not necessarily real; there may be no truth in it. The wealthy are creating a smokescreen to provoke chaos and confusion. Do not be deceived. Sin has become a culture. The Bible tells us that we cannot serve God and money (Matt. 6:24). Whatever you place more worth on becomes your idol (WOR-SHIP). Idolatry is making anything worth more than God. Anything more valuable than God is worthless.

We are living in the last days. The global pandemic, caused by what appears to be an engineered virus, COVID-19, has managed to cause international lockdowns, border closings, widespread business closures, economic collapse, and massive unemployment. This has amounted to an unprecedented curtailment of civil liberties and freedoms to keep people safe by locking them up in their homes, along with vaccine mandates. We find ourselves living in a world that is increasingly ruled not by our democratic systems and institutions but by public health fiat, carried out by our democratic politicians who rule by instilling fear and panic. Millions of people are dying at an astronomical rate. Of every disease and sickness that we know to cause death, such as high blood pressure, blood poisoning, breast cancer, pancreatic cancer, inflammation of the kidney; colon, rectal and anal cancers, pneumonia, influenza, diabetes, obesity, suicide, HIV, lung cancer, stroke, and other cerebrovascular diseases, somehow, we ONLY now hear of one type of death—the infamous coronavirus, aka COVID-19.

As you can see, death comes in many forms. Do not let death catch you unprepared. Death gets its power from sin. You awaken death by disobeying God. When you do wrong, you activate death, but when you enter the Kingdom of God, you kill death. Christ decided to carry out the sentence for our sin on Himself, so we would not have to *die twice!* Man is made up of spirit, soul, and body. Your spirit is the real you; your soul is your mind, will, and emotions, and your body is your earth suit. Your earth suit will eventually die, but your spirit man will continue to live. Hebrews 9:27 states, "Just as it is appointed and destined for all men to die once and after this comes judgment."

God is our Father because He is our Source. It is because of Him that we live and move and have our beings. We have rebelled against God, therefore separating ourselves from our Source. When a plant is pulled out of the soil, you don't have to stomp it to kill it. The plant will eventually die because it was separated from what makes it alive: its source—the soil. When you pull a fish out of the ocean, you don't have to kill it. It will eventually die because it is no longer connected to its source—the ocean. Therefore, when we who were created by God, in the image of God, become separated from our Source, we too will eventually die because we are no longer connected to the Source. When we violate God's law, we will automatically suffer the consequences.

Every one of us has made bad choices in our lives. God does not care about the mistakes or bad choices you made five years ago, two years ago, or one week ago. He is not even concerned if it was yesterday. God only wants to know—*What choice will you make today?* He said in Hebrew 3:7, "Today, if you will hear my voice, do not harden your heart."

There are two kingdoms—the Kingdom of God (Light) and the Kingdom of Darkness. You are in one or the other; there are no in-betweens. The goal of life is for you to meet the Light (Christ) so that you won't die in your darkness. Deuteronomy 30:19 states, "I have set before you, life and death, blessing and cursing. Therefore, choose life … for God alone is your life and the length of your days."

You are in the fight whether you want to be or not, so choose your Kingdom. Wake up, people! If you remain on the Titanic listening to the music, you will die.

Jesus came to Earth to give us back what was stolen from Adam (the first human man and father of all mankind) in the Garden of Eden and ensure that we don't have to die twice. Adam spiritually died in the garden when he disobeyed God. And the only way to rectify Adam's disobedience was for Jesus (the 2nd Adam having perfect and pure blood) to come and die for all mankind. When we accept Him as our

Lord and Savior and make a conscious decision to live according to the laws of the Kingdom of Heaven, realizing that He paid the ultimate and perfect sacrifice to buy back our lives after Adam handed them over to Satan, we will NOT die twice. You should not be caught dead without knowing your sins are forgiven. Life is short, death is sure, and hell is real. Let's pray the following prayer out loud.

Lord God, Creator of Heaven and Earth,

Thank you for all you do for me. By faith, I believe Jesus is the son of God, and He came and paid a debt I could not pay. Jesus died for my sins, so I will not have to die twice. I believe He died on the cross for my sins and rose the third day for my justification to give me back my rights as a citizen of Heaven and the right to rule and have dominion in the earth. Father, forgive me for my sins, known and unknown. I renounce any and every sin (call out the specific sins) *in my life that exalts itself against the knowledge of God.*

I receive Christ as my Lord and Saviour and make a conscious decision to live according to the laws of the Kingdom of Heaven. I submit my will to You and say, 'Lord, not my will, but Your will be done in my life.' In Christ's name, Amen.

As John the Baptist would declare, *"Repent, confess your sin (known and unknown), acknowledge Jesus Christ as Lord and Savior, and be baptized to receive the gift of the Holy Spirit, for the KINGDOM OF GOD IS AT HAND!"* Make a conscious decision to live according to the laws, statutes, and commandments of the Kingdom of Heaven.

NOTES

CHAPTER TWELVE

THE PRODIGAL SON

The prodigal son, mentioned in Luke 15:11, was the foolish son in one of Christ's parables who asked for an early inheritance and subsequently squandered it on wild living in another country. When famine hit, he got a job feeding the pigs in the field. His hunger was so great that he even craved their food. He thought to himself, *"What in the world have I gotten myself into? I had everything I needed at home. I was so blessed. I had no idea how blessed I was with my father. I sinned and rebelled against the one person who provided and protected me. I thought there was something in the world I was missing, and now I have come to realize that there is nothing in the world but misery. It appears to be good, but the end is devastation and even death."*

Luke 15:11-32

The prodigal son realized that even his father's hired men had food to spare. He longed for home and was determined to return and work as a servant. The repentant son expressed how unworthy he was to be his father's son, but he was met with his father's unconditional love and forgiveness and was restored to his place in the family. This son had come to a place where he *couldn't breathe.* He had sunken to a very low level.

Does this sound like someone you might know? This sounds a lot like God's chosen people. We came from a place of moral standards and honor, and now, we have sunken to a very low place. Let's be like the prodigal son and remember our God. Let's remember who we are (God's chosen people) and repent to be met with the Father's unconditional love and forgiveness.

Daniel's Prayer of Forgiveness for Israel

And I prayed unto the LORD my God, and made my confession, and said, O Lord, the great and dreadful God, keeping the covenant and mercy to them that love him, and to them that keep his commandments; We have sinned, and have committed iniquity, and have done wickedly, and have rebelled, even by departing from thy precepts and from thy judgments: Neither have we hearkened unto thy servants the prophets, which spoke in thy name to our kings, our princes, and our fathers, and to all the people of the land.

O Lord, righteousness belongeth unto thee, but unto us confusion of faces, as at this day; to the men of Judah, and to the inhabitants of Jerusalem, and unto all Israel, that are near, and that are far off, through all the countries whither thou hast driven them, because of their trespass that they have trespassed against thee. O Lord, to us belongeth confusion of face, to our kings, to our princes, and to our fathers, because we have sinned against thee. To the Lord our God belong mercies and forgiveness, though we have rebelled against him; Neither have we obeyed the voice of the LORD our God, to walk in his laws, which he set before us by his servants the prophets.

Yea, all Israel have transgressed thy law, even by departing, that they might not obey thy voice; therefore, the curse is poured upon us, and the oath that is written in the law of Moses the servant of God, because we have sinned against him. And he hath confirmed his words, which he spake against us, and against our judges that judged us, by bringing upon us a great evil: for under the whole heaven hath not been done as hath been done upon Jerusalem. As it is written in the law of Moses, all this evil is come upon us: yet made we not our prayer before the LORD our God, that we might turn from our iniquities, and understand thy truth. Therefore, hath the LORD watched upon the evil, and brought it upon us: for the LORD our God is righteous in all his works which he doeth: for we obeyed not his voice.

And now, O Lord our God, that hast brought thy people forth out of the land of Egypt with a mighty hand, and hast gotten thee renown, as at this day; we have sinned, we have done wickedly. O Lord, according to all thy righteousness, I beseech thee, let thine anger and thy fury be turned away from thy city Jerusalem, thy holy mountain: because for our sins, and for the iniquities of our fathers, Jerusalem and thy people are become a reproach to all that are about us. Now therefore, O our God, hear the prayer of thy servant, and his supplications, and cause thy face to shine upon thy sanctuary that is desolate, for the Lord's sake. O my God, incline thine ear, and hear; open thine eyes, and behold our desolations, and the city which is called by thy name: for we do not present our supplications before thee for our righteousness, but for thy great mercies. O Lord, hear; O Lord, forgive; O Lord, hearken and do; defer not, for thine own sake, O my God: for thy city and thy people are called by thy name.

Daniel 9:1-19

CHAPTER THIRTEEN

MY JOURNEY

As far back as I can remember, I've had an ardent fascination with Black people and culture. As a young Black girl, I took pride in my Black heritage. I often thanked God for being birthed in a Black family, despite our struggles. Growing up, Black people had a strong sense of culture and community. As a culture, some activities occurred naturally, and then there were certain things that Black people just didn't do. As a culture, Black people believed in God, most even went to church, and those who did not at least believed in Jesus Christ. We did not play with the devil, and we NEVER dabbled into anything that appeared evil. All these things constantly pondered in my mind. I now realize that this was the God gene that kept us upholding moral standards.

Throughout the years, I bought and read books on the history of Blacks. As a result, I developed a passion for Black history.

My passion for Black history birthed this desire to open a Youth Center to teach Black history to Black youth. I realized that most of our children have no knowledge of the legacy of Martin Luther King, Malcolm X, Frederic Douglas, and others. For example, I found out in my older years that Frederic Douglas wrote a profound piece of literature referencing the 4th of July. After coming across this knowledge, I no longer celebrate the 4th of July. Douglas stated:

This 4th of July is yours, not mine. You may rejoice; I must mourn. For you to ask us to join you in celebration is "inhuman mockery and sacrilegious irony." "What, to the American slave, is your 4th of July? I answer: a day that reveals to him, more than all other days in the year, the gross injustice and cruelty to which he is the constant victim. If we celebrate the fourth of July, it would be treason, most scandalous and shocking, and would make me a reproach before God and the world. To him, your celebration is a sham; your boasted liberty, an unholy license; your national greatness, swelling vanity; your sound of rejoicing is empty and heartless. There is not a nation on the earth guilty of practices more shocking and bloodier than are the people of the United States, at this very hour.

At this time, I was still not aware that our history started in the Bible. I begin via the Holy Spirit, coming across all types of literature on the fact that we are the people of the Bible. I was so eager to celebrate the excellence of Black people. I was certain that if we, as a culture, could understand where we came from, we could change our trajectory.

While excited about our Black excellence, I was equally perplexed. I wondered, "How can a group of people be so EXEMPLARY in all endeavors yet exist in a perpetual state of degradation? Why are our Black women so rare, beautiful, and exotic but consistently displayed by the media as fat, ugly, and oversexualized? Why are we creators but not owners? How do we dominate and excel above all other races in any sport we attempt? These are the questions that consumed me.

And it didn't stop. I pondered about the soulful, melodic voices with which our Black people have been so naturally blessed and the allure of the Black man by not only Black women but women of all ethnicities. My heart knew there was something special about us. Finally, in 2003, I asked the Lord, "Father, what is it about Black people?"

And the intentionality behind my journey began! The Holy Spirit led me to all types of literature claiming that Black people were, in fact, the people of the Bible. One day, my nephew sent me a Youtube video of Pastor Stephen Darby. He was such an honorable man with a beautiful family who would BRING IT!

A true scholar and disciple, Pastor Darby taught a message titled, "Negroland." He confirmed that Black people are the chosen people of God, and everything he said resonated in my spirit. I listened to more and more messages from Pastor Darby, which further watered the groundwork that God had already laid on my heart. Every time I listened to one of his teachings, it was hot off the press—an anointed, "right now" word, no matter how old the message. Unfortunately, Pastor Darby is no longer with us, but I love this man of God. He was an awesome and profound teacher who was not afraid to speak the truth.

I also watched the teachings of Pastor Omar Thibeaux of Louisiana. Pastor Omar brought a 22-series teaching titled, "Edom: The Roots of Rome;" it is a MUST watch. This is an awesome series consisting of in-depth research. He provides a complete and thorough timeline of who we are as the children of Israel and who is Esau (our enemy). Last, the Holy Spirit led me to the Gathering of Christ Church (GOCC), which can be found on YouTube. Their core belief is, "Christ is the way the man should follow to receive the Kingdom of the Most High. The body of Christ is not a building made by hands, for the Spirit of the Most High God cannot be contained in one place, but the body of Christ is, in fact, those who are baptized into His Spirit. We are living in a time in which the Most High is gathering His elect to the elect, with their role being a voice and sign proclaiming the truth, showing prophecy, revealing those in power against the elect, and spiritually preparing for the last stand with the elect against the forces of evil."

GOCC relates everyday occurrences and events to what the Bible says about these "last days." The church has an honorable group of elders who have a love and passion for their mission to gather God's people in preparation for the return of our Lord and Savior, Jesus Christ. They have gathered together several resources, known and unknown, to quantify the true history of our people, rightly dividing the word of God.

I have no doubt in my heart, mind, and soul that we are the children of promise, according to the Bible. My passion is that you come to know this same truth.

THE ISRAELITE MAN

Who is the Black Man?
He is a man of Valor
He is a man of Honor
He outshines all other men
He is created in the image of the Creator
He is sealed with the embodiment of the Creator
He is a King and a Priest
His value is of Great Price
He is a diamond in the rough
He has the courage of a Lion
He is a Protector of his family
He is every woman's desire
He is bad to the bone
Everything he puts his mind and hands to do will be
Blessed
And those that fear him know his value
That is why he is hunted down and trodden under-
foot
His enemy's jealousy has spilled over to a murderous
heart
But he has forgotten his worth
He has forgotten his purpose
Some of you have lost your way,
Some of you have been consumed (brainwashed) by
the world
Return, Oh Man of Valor and take your rightful
place.

FINAL WORDS FROM THE AUTHOR

I hope after reading this book, you have come to the knowledge of the truth that has been kept from you, and that truth is that you are God's chosen people. Just because you have no knowledge of certain information or have never heard anyone speak on a particular matter does not mean the information is not true. Usually, when we hear the truth about something for the first time, we reject it because it is unfamiliar. It's sad to think of how many people, especially our people, are lost because they cannot receive and accept the truth when it is presented to them. The Bible informs us that many will not accept the truth. Hosea 4:6 states, "My people are destroyed for lack of knowledge; because thou hast rejected knowledge, I will also reject thee … seeing thou hast forgotten the law of thy God, I will also forget my children." This scripture does not refer to all people; it ONLY refers to those brought into this country by slave ships and indigenous people, who Americans want to call "Indians," who were already here.

We are the people of this Bible and those referenced in Hosea 4:6. We have been denied knowledge and information more than any other people group. If you think that scripture is not referring to us, think again. We have been constantly abused, exploited, killed, and destroyed by other nations and America, which the book Revelation refers to as Babylon. We are the children of the Most High God. Although one must be born again, this has nothing to do with your salvation. It has everything to do with our bloodline, being that we are the actual ancestors of Abraham, Isaac, and Jacob, OUR forefathers. I know this is a shocker for most.

Understand that we are fighting a psychological, spiritual battle. When we learn who we are, the elites lose power. They don't want us to wake up. Remember the movie with Eddie Murphy, Trading Places? This is what happened to us. We were switched. Why? Because our people, all through the Bible and even now, turned away from God and began to practice pagan rituals and worship pagan gods. God allowed our enemy to rule over us. Hence, why the LORD said what He said in Hosea 6:4. The Bible tells us that God despised Esau because he was fleshly and didn't reason well. Esau (Edomites) set out to change himself into us from the onset. They erased us, our black pictures, and our history. Esau will rule until

Christ's return, but we do not have to remain in our present condition.

The Beast System (Rome/American Government) has been designed to destroy us to bring us to a place where we can't breathe. The economy, sports, Hollywood, the educational system, welfare, the feminist movement, Eugenic or Planned Parenthood, medical institutes, and ghettos have all been designed to perpetuate the plight of Black Americans. We have been living our lives in accordance with soap operas, Love and Hip Hop, and other reality shows in this *"Beast System."* Romans 12:2 advises, "Be not conformed to this world, but be ye transformed by the renewing of your mind." However, we have been psychologically programmed, via social engineering, with years of subliminal messages via television, music, intimidation, domination, and manipulation, constantly showing negative images of Black people. This is on purpose and by design. We are evidence of a crime, and the elite powers are trying to hide and eliminate the evidence.

We think we are the worst of the worst because we believe we are the worst. Our sin keeps us in our worsened state. We were mind-raped, which caused us to adopt *their image* of our God, which bounds us to slavery.

The Bible speaks of us being a stiff-necked people. We have been so conditioned to the lies of this world about who we are that when we tell our people the truth, they won't allow themselves to have an open mind to hear the truth. The Bible says you will know the truth, and the truth will make you free. Christ said, "I am the way, the truth, and the life." The question is, do we want to know the truth? For most of us, the answer is no. Why? Because we want to remain in our low, depressing, ignorant state.

Our people are chasing everything under the sun except The Most High. This is why awakening our people to the truth MUST BE PRIORITY for those who seek and know the truth. We have been hijacked and sold a lie. Everything is a lie! America is a lie! Black people, wake up! It's time to repent and come out of sin.

The Christian church often prays and talks of the Great Awakening for America. Black people, WE are that "Great Awakening." God is waking up His people in these last days so that we CAN BREATHE AND BE SAVED FROM A HELLISH WORLD AND A BURNING HELL!

Understand this one thing—The Most High chose US! He could have chosen any other nation, but HE CHOSE US! And although we turned our back on him, committed adultery, and fornicated with other gods, HE NEVER GAVE UP ON US!

1 Kings 10:9 states, "Blessed be the LORD thy God, which delighted in thee, to set thee on the throne of Israel: because the LORD loved Israel forever." Black Americans, repent and return to

YOUR God, our Father; this is a matter of Life and Death. Deuteronomy 30:19 states, "I have set before you, life and death, therefore choose life ... that both thou and thy seed may live."

Open your eyes and look around. Who has been targeted and destroyed since being kidnapped and dragged to America? Answer: Black Americans. Think it not strange what is happening? These are the last days! America has nothing to offer you but death. He who has an ear to hear, let him hear. We have sinned and turned away from the Most High God, therefore, been relegated to a state of *"I can't breathe."*

NOTES

CONNECT WITH THE AUTHOR

Thank you for reading, *I Can't Breathe: Don't Die Twice.* Deborah looks forward to connecting with you. Here are a few ways you can connect with the author and stay updated on new releases, speaking engagements, products, and more.

EMAIL   deblaster@outlook.com

Made in the USA
Columbia, SC
31 March 2023

75459de6-5803-451c-a6b3-d177233f7982R01